*To [redacted]
Happy Birthday!
Nick Rizzo*

Kids Party Magic

The Guide to Stress-Free, Fun-Filled Birthdays for Little Hosts and Big Fun!

Dr. Nicholas Rizzo

Kids Party Magic
The Guide to Stress-Free, Fun-Filled Birthdays for Little Hosts and Big Fun!

Copyright © 2023 by Nicholas Rizzo

Nicholas Rizzo
7270 W College Dr, Ste 102
Palos Heights IL 60463-1879
Email: rizzomagic@aol.com
Website: www.kidspartymagic.info

All rights reserved. No part of this book may be reproduced, stored in a retrieval system, or transmitted by any means, electronic, mechanical, photocopying, recording, or otherwise, without prior written permission from the author except for brief quotations embodied in critical articles or reviews and certain noncommercial uses permitted by copyright law.

Any Internet addresses (websites, blogs, products, companies, etc.), services and products (party products, foods, etc.) referenced in this book are offered as a resource and are not intended in any way to be or imply an endorsement. This publication contains the opinions and ideas of the author. The ideas and suggestions in this book may not be suitable for every individual or every situation and are not guaranteed or warrantied to produce any particular or specific results. The author expressly disclaims any liability, loss, or risk, personal or otherwise incurred as a direct or indirect consequence of the use or application of the contents of this book.

Paperback ISBN-13: 978-0-9748220-4-4
E-book ISBN: 978-0-9748220-9-9
LCCN: 2023917441

Printed in the United States of America

Contents

Introduction………………………………………………	1
What's the Best Age to Have a Party?……………...…….....	2
Planning…………………………………………….	3
Don't Go It Alone…………………………………….	5
Other Parents Attending……………………………..	6
Internet and Social Media……………………………	7
Choosing a Theme……………………………………	8
Choosing a Time and Date…………………………..	11
Budgeting…………………………………………….	12
Location……………………………………………...	13
Professional Entertainers……………………………..	15
Guest List…………………………………………….	17
Invitations……………………………………………	18
Party Supplies……………………………………….	21
Decorations………………………………………….	22
Birthday Child Siblings……………………………..	24
Kids with Special Needs…………………………….	25
Age-by-Age………………………………………….	26
Safety First………………………………………….	27
The Party Schedule…………………………………	28
Just Before the Party………………………………..	30
Arrival Activities and Free Play…………………….	31
Games and Group Activities………………………..	33
Refreshments……………………………………….	34
Cake & Ice Cream…………………………………..	37
Gift Opening………………………………………..	39
Farewell Activities………………………………….	41
Party Favors………………………………………..	42
After the Party……………………………………..	44
Thank You Notes…………………………………..	45
Finally………………………………………………	46

Kids Party Magic Planning Guide (Invitation Checklist, Timeline, Budget, Shopping List, Gift Wish List, Vendor List, Guest List, Notes)

Introduction

Parties are a great opportunity to create some beautiful memories. It won't be long until your child thinks they are too old for parties or want to hang out with friends. Enjoy the birthday cake while you can. But almost all parents are short on time, energy, or finances. Sometimes preparing for the party looms so large that we have mixed emotions and lose sight of the event's purpose – your child's party.

This book will help first-time, busy, or burned-out parents find answers to their questions and find interesting and inspiring ideas. It will remove the guesswork, so you don't over-produce, obsess, or under-prepare. The purpose here is to create a successful, stress-free event, enhancing the fun for you and your children. It's not about impressing other parents but about making the day memorable for your child and their guests.

What's the Best Age to Have a Party?

Consider your child's age, maturity, temperament, desire to be social and things like family attendance or involvement. If throwing a party for a one or two-year-old, make it more of an adult gathering and don't expect the child to be interested. You'll want to keep the attention off the young child and schedule it around nap and feeding schedules.

For three-year-olds, keep the parties simple – they'll appreciate fancier parties with themes and planned activities later. Something simple like a play date may be all that's needed. Invite only a few children along with their parents. At this age, expect the children to be more interested in parallel play and individual interests instead of a traditional structured birthday party. Let parents be with their children and respond to their fun or waning attention.

Around four or five years is a good age to have a birthday party centered around the child – they have started to have specific friends and have developed tastes in foods and toys. This is a great age to involve the birthday child in planning the party, especially in picking the theme. This is also an appropriate age if hiring professional entertainment.

Planning

The most important piece of advice here is to plan ahead. Doing things at the last minute creates stress, can incur extra costs, and increases the chances of things going wrong.

> ### Quick Tips
> - Planning ahead is the key to a stress-free party.
> - Planning allows you to focus on one task at a time.

If your child is at least four or five years old, one of the best ways to make your child's party successful is to let them help plan the party. While you shouldn't let them make all the decisions, involving your child may make the big day more enjoyable. Even the youngest children have preferences and can help pick a theme – a three-year-old who loves animals will love a jungle, zoo, or puppy party. The four-year-old who likes building may like a construction or truck-themed party. Children aged seven to ten will have more definite ideas.

The first step is to develop a timeline for the party. Fifteen to twenty minutes now may save you hours later. Start planning four to six weeks before the party. This lets you pull the party together at a relaxed pace and eliminate stress. For example, this extra time will allow you to purchase party supplies as part of regular shopping trips instead of having to run around at the last minute. The most considerable risk with waiting until the last minute is a very important one: some of your child's friends, or even their best friend, may be unable to attend due to other commitments. If you cannot plan that far ahead, don't worry too much because the party will usually turn out okay, and the kids won't know or care that it was a last-minute thing.

Prioritize the most important things. If you overbuy and overdo, you may have extra work, extra cost, and less fun. If you do as much ahead of time as possible, then you won't be in a time crunch if something unexpected comes up the week before the party. For example, suppose you prepare the party favors and activities a couple of weeks ahead. Then, you can spend the days before the party on the things that should be done closer to party time, like food and decorations.

Make as many checklists as you need. Utilize the Timeline, Budget, Shopping List, Gift Wish List, Vendor List, and Guest List templates at the end of this book. The Shopping List includes decorations, favors, and snacks. Make a "Day of Party To-Do" list along with who will be helping with them. Use the Guest List for RSVPs with space to write any notes and the gifts given next to guests' names.

If you have family or friends helping, feel free to delegate appropriately. For example, write down and identify the things you can have someone else do. Make a list of things you must do yourself because they can't be outsourced or delegated, they're expensive, or they're things you want to do because they'll be fun – like making invitations with your child.

Have backup plans for each type of possible failure. Have plans for guests that don't show and guests that show up with extra siblings. Be prepared for vendor cancellations, food and beverage shortages, and inclement weather. For example, do activities in the garage in case of rain or play a video if the entertainer doesn't show. Have extra activities and games planned in case some don't pan out well or hold the children's interest. Be prepared with an additional adult to watch shy or wandering children, especially when plans change.

Don't Go It Alone

You'd be amazed at how even a little help can go a long way. The younger the guests and the more of them, the more important this is. Potential helpers include family, friends, neighbors, parents of guests, and paid vendors like entertainers, caterers, and even maid services.

First, compare your list of things to do with your list of volunteers and look for unmistakable choices. An aunt who likes to cook can bake cupcakes the day before, even if you arrange them into a cupcake cake later. An artistic older sibling may help decorate or supervise arrival activities. Some adults who would otherwise be uninterested in helping may be interested if it's in a way that interests them. A relative that likes photography may be a good choice to take pictures during the party. Someone who is not the best with children can go shopping or pick up the cake or balloons.

Lastly, assign tasks to people that want to help but have no specific interests or can do given jobs at the time of the party. Other parents or adult guests can help with activities, serve refreshments, and make a list of who gives what gift for reference in Thank You notes later. Cleanup may be quite a task. It may be worthwhile to delegate small tasks. Have the older brother vacuum and have the older sister help with any dishes – don't assign a mountain of tasks to one person. Consider a "labor exchange." Agree with another parent or family member to help at their party if they help at yours. But be sure to keep any commitments made. If using vendors or caterers, use trusted ones you have used before.

To stay organized, jot down who is assigned each task, but don't get into conflict if something doesn't go right or get done, as that will affect the party atmosphere. No party goes off perfectly; expect something to go wrong.

Other Parents Attending

Parents usually expect to stay if their child is four or younger. Otherwise, parents assume it's up to them whether they stay for the party. They usually drop their kids off between the ages of six and seven.

One important consideration is space and venue. If having the party at a home with limited space, include attending parents in the final head count. If having the party at a venue, find out if the venue allows parents to stay and if there is an extra charge per person. If you're hosting a drop-off party, be sure to include that on the invitation. If you need extra supervision or help for the party or want parents to stay for the party, discuss it when you accept the RSVP.

Sometimes you may be faced with an uninvited adult or parent that insists on staying despite space limitations or other issues. The only choices here are to invite them in or to turn them away, giving them a polite explanation as to why. Remember you're the host, and smile either way. If problems arise, consider not inviting them to the next party. Lastly, as they are guests also, have something for the adults to eat.

Internet and Social Media

Social media can be a double-edged sword. Use the Internet to find ideas and party planning, but don't be fooled into thinking things like "bigger is better" or being urged to buy more stuff that's not needed.

Don't look to social media and think that you must compete with other parents or find approval. Don't post the date of the party or post an open invitation announcement on social media as it may result in hurt feelings of those not coming, uninvited guests, or even create issues with ex-spouses.

During the party unplug from social media. Keep your phone on for emergencies but turn off notifications. Consider saving vendor websites and contact info on your phone. Keep in mind that some parents may not be fond of having their child photographed, and especially not fond of pictures of their child on social media or websites.

Choosing a Theme

Choosing a theme makes planning easier and makes the party more fun – decisions about what kind of invitations, activities, and decorations become almost self-evident.

If your child is four years old or older, one of the most essential ways to involve them is to let them help to choose a theme. Start about a month or two beforehand by browsing at party stores, toy stores, party aisles of larger stores, and talking with other parents about previous parties your child has attended. Offer some suggestions and be prepared to adapt to a more practical theme if necessary. For example, if you can't manage a real Pirate adventure at the beach, work out a compromise, like a Pirate-themed Pool Party.

The number of guests, type of location, and your budget can all influence the theme. For example, if you have limited room at your house, consider what local party destinations lend themselves to which themes. A beach could go with Pirates, Under the Sea, Mermaids, Boats, etc. If you want to invite many people and can only spend a little money, a nearby park would suggest a Picnic Party, Sports, or Safari. Also, consider the ages and genders of your guests. In case your guests are primarily adults at a first or second Birthday, or children of various ages and genders, select a theme that all could relate to or at least have fun with.

Select a theme that fits your child's likes and personality. First or second Birthday themes can focus on the number "1" or "2" or a child's favorite character, toy, book, movie, or television show. If your child is high-energy, an outdoor Sports Party with many games would be great. Calmer themes such as Teddy or Tea Party might be better if your child is quiet or shy.

Some themes come up at parties over and over in the same year, especially if wildly popular in the movies or tv shows. But if your child is interested in it, stick with the preferred theme – but create an imaginative aspect, such as a new, unique activity or giveaway.

If the party theme is a specific character or story, such as Harry Potter™, Blue's Clues™, or Barbie™, even though it may sound unlikely in today's electronic age, don't assume every child will be familiar with it. You can set the stage beforehand by sending out creative invitations or electronic/e-mail invitations that include a link to a video introducing the character or party theme. You can even create QR codes online for a website or online video.

For sports themes, see if there is a venue that would support the theme. For example, if the child admires dad's golf game, hold the party at a miniature golf venue. Even if your child wants a Karate party, avoid any themes relating to combat sports, as it may lead to injuries and upset parents.

Some holidays are more fun for children than others, and if your child's birthday is near a holiday, it may lend itself to a children's party surprisingly well. Holiday themes are also perfect for school parties and sometimes lend themselves to educational opportunities. Some holiday themes include New Year's Eve, Chinese New Year, Cinco de Mayo, Easter, Valentine's Day, Mardi Gras, and Halloween. On the other hand, if the birthday is near a gift-giving or revered holiday such as Christmas, it may be better to celebrate it separately.

Feel free to expand the party's theme to appeal to more guests. If your child likes Firefighters, make it a "Rescue Heroes" party with a Police and Rescue Team theme. If your child wants Batman™, then have a Superheroes party and let the guests bring one of their toys or action figures of their favorite hero with them. (But be sure to keep track of any toys guests bring.) To build anticipation for the guests, think of a catchy name for the theme and use it on the invitations. For example, if having a Cowboy-themed party, you could use "Wild, Wild, West" or "Ride 'em, Cowboys." Call a Science-themed party a "Mad Scientist" party, a Zoo-themed party "Go Bananas" or "Safari Adventure". A trip to a children's farm could be an "Old MacDonald Party," and a Valentine-themed party a "Sweetheart" party.

Some general ideas for themes include:

- Aliens
- Airplanes
- Artists
- Avengers™
- Baby Shark™
- Baking
- Barbie™
- Barnyard
- Batman™
- Beach Party
- Beauty Parlor
- Blues Clues™
- Camp Out
- Cars™
- Carnival
- Circus
- Clifford™
- County Fair
- Construction
- Dance
- Disney Princess™
- Detective
- Dinosaurs
- Dolls
- Dr. Suess™
- Dress-up
- 50's Party
- Flower Power
- Finding Nemo™
- Fire Fighter
- First Birthday
- Fortnite™
- Frozen™
- Gaming
- Gardening
- Glam
- Harry Potter™
- Hot Wheels™
- Ice Cream Parlor
- Jungle Safari
- Knights
- Lego™
- Lion King™
- Luau
- Magic
- Mermaid
- Moana™
- Monster Truck
- Movies
- Music
- Mystery
- Nature
- Paw Patrol™
- Pirates
- Pizza Party
- Pool Party
- Rainbow
- Robots
- Sesame Street™
- Science

– Kids Party Magic –

- Slime Making
- Slumber Party
- Spa
- Space/Astronauts
- Spiderman™
- Super Mario™
- Superman™
- Star Wars™
- Tea Party
- Teddy Bear
- Toy Story™
- Trains
- Trolls
- Under the Sea
- Unicorn
- Weird Science
- Willy Wonka™
- Wizards
- Wonder Woman™

Choosing a Time and Date

Try to have the party on the weekend as close to the child's birthday as possible. But do your best to select a date your child's best friend can attend. It's better to choose another date than not have the birthday child's best friend or favorite family member there. Changing the date by several weeks is acceptable to avoid busy holidays if the child understands. Friday afternoon and midday, Saturday, and Sunday parties are good choices, but all have pros and cons. Fridays are good because the midday party takes up a weekday, and everyone has the rest of the weekend for other activities. If you choose Saturday to have a party, you can use Sunday to relax and recover. Sunday afternoon parties have fewer scheduling conflicts, and you have all day Saturday to prepare. Be sure to hold Sunday parties at noon or later to reduce conflicts with religious obligations.

Consider the age of the children and choose a time of day when they are typically at their best temperament. Many younger children are more pleasant in the morning and get more difficult in the afternoon and evening. A morning party or two hours around lunch is a good choice. Know that you may have more late arrivals or no-shows in the early morning. Make sure to end the party to avoid any pre-naptime difficulties. Consider if you will be providing a full meal or not – if not, you should start the party an hour or more after typical mealtimes and end an hour before, typically between 2 p.m. and 5 p.m. On the other hand, if you must have the party between 11 a.m. to 1 p.m. or 5 p.m. to 7 p.m., you should provide a meal. Otherwise, you only need adequate snacks and the anticipated cake and ice cream.

Budgeting

You don't need to break the bank to have a great party. Some parents go overboard, thinking "more is better" or that they must compete with other parents when it's never the case. Don't try to outdo other parents. Don't give in to your child's demands, comparisons with other parties, or unrealistic images on the Internet.

The bottom line is that it's about making your child feel special, independent of how much money you spend. For example, it's usually more important that each guest has a small, thoughtful favor to take home rather than a giant goody bag of cheap toys or favors that the guest child will discard in a few days.

> ### Quick Tips
> - Plan your menu at the same time you plan your budget.
> - The more you budget, the fewer surprise expenses.
> - Compare prices online.
> - Success of a party isn't dependent on the amount spent.

Buy only what you want, need, and can afford. Focus on decorating for the biggest impact for money spent. A good rule of thumb is $15 to $30 per child, but having a party for less is possible. Add up the costs for the required items like cake, ice cream, favors, and decorations. Keep in mind that costs can quickly escalate if you must pay for a location, hire an entertainer, serve a full meal, and give expensive prizes and favor bags.

There are a lot of ways to save on costs. Some all-inclusive party destinations can be pricey. You'll have to weigh priorities and see if letting the venue do the work for you is more cost-effective. Compare prices of different venues. Be smart about buying your party supplies. Look for items on sale throughout the year. Check clearance aisles when shopping. Look for bargains at big chain discount stores and dollar stores. Buy favors in bulk packs or sets. Use crafts an arrival activity that can be taken home as favors. Buy food and beverages in bulk. When ordering online, compare prices and shipping costs between websites. Avoid impulse purchasing, omit unnecessary extras, and beware of overpriced partyware packages. If you're on a tight budget, keep the party short and small, and have the party during a time of day when you aren't expected to provide a full meal.

Location

Just as when choosing a theme, there are things to think about when deciding where to have the party. Consider the age of the birthday child, the number of children, the number of adults, and the theme. For example, the best places for First or Second Birthdays are where your child is familiar and comfortable, such as your home or a relative's home. Consider safety issues, especially as it relates to the age of the guests. For example, a Pool Party is not safe for a gathering of 25 two-year-olds. Avoid party environments with stairs, balconies, high windows, large glass doors, or busy streets. Remember that children can be unpredictable in strange environments, particularly with the excitement of a party.

There are pros and cons to having a party at your home, but more often the pros outweigh the cons. Consider if your home is amenable to the type of party you're having. It may accommodate a larger crowd if it has a large play area or a large, finished basement. If it doesn't, consider having the party at a relative or friend's home. Don't worry about what others may think as not everyone will like your home or furniture. Remember, the kids will not remember how big or fancy your house is, but they will remember the good time they had with their friends. Some advantages to having a party at home include having plenty of time to set up, having your supplies close at hand, having the party where your child is comfortable, no unsanitary public restrooms, and the guest's children are safe. Disadvantages to a home party include cleaning your house before and after the party, the risk of damage to your house, and possible space limitations.

If a family member or friend who lives nearby offers their home, help decorate and offer to pay for a housekeeper afterward. If a family member offers their pool, hire a certified lifeguard. Be sure to clarify which parts of the home the children will be allowed to use. Be sure you are on the same page regarding other aspects of the party, like locking up pets, removing easily broken valuables, parking, etc.

As with home parties, venues, or locations away from home have advantages and disadvantages. Venues may lend to a specific theme. Some may include entertainment, refreshments, setup, and cleanup all into one. But don't think your work is done if you opt for a location away from home. Plan it as thoroughly as if it were at home. Take into consideration all the pros and cons, like whether you will get to come home to a clean house, and that off-site parties are usually better for children five years and older as younger children may be upset by strange surroundings. Some venues have time limits for the party to allow for the next group of partygoers.

Look around your community – many places have space you can rent or use at no or little cost. Sometimes the venue lends itself to a theme. Ideas here include Amusement Parks, Arcades, Baby/toddler gym, Baseball Games, a Beach, Bounce Gyms, Bowling, Build-A-Bear Workshop™, Children's Farm, Craft Store, Firehouse, Go-cart Racing, Miniature Golf, Movies, Museum, Nature Center, Park, Pool, Themed or Kid-friendly Restaurants, Roller Skating, Theaters, Video Arcade, Water Parks, and the Zoo. Some facilities like magic shops or theaters have special children's party packages. Different venues may provide food, staff, favors, and other services and supplies. Choose a venue that's within 15 to 20 minutes travel time for most guests.

If you end up with many guests, consider an outdoor venue. Public parks are often good choices because they're usually free or inexpensive. Disadvantages to parks include that it's a pain to haul all the party supplies to the park, the park may be crowded or booked, and you may need help finding a space for your party. If you have a party at a park, it is critical to reserve or stake out an area or send someone early to claim an area with a shelter. Know that most parks require reservations or permits. If your party is outdoors, go with easily servable refreshments like pizza, and activities like team sports. Always have a "rain plan."

If choosing a larger venue or if you have a lot of guests, be sure to have enough adult volunteers as supervisors. As children are trained to "listen to adults," adult background conversations can be a distraction to children. If there are many adults, have a separate room for non-supervising adults to socialize. Given the family nature of the day, play it safe and avoid alcohol in front of the children.

Most venues will have vendor agreements or contracts. Be sure to read them in their entirety, especially any fine print. If you are unsure of the meaning of something in the contract, or if there is too much legal jargon, run it by an attorney. Some are upfront about costs; others may roll added expenses into the final price tag. Be sure to discuss costs upfront, getting quotes in writing if possible. You don't want any surprises that would impact the success of the party.

Professional Entertainers

There are a few advantages to hiring a professional children's entertainer. Some party themes beg for a professional entertainer – a magic party begs to have a magician. (On the other hand, no one expects a unicorn to attend a unicorn party.) An entertainer may help when you are short of time. Entertainers can usually come direct to you wherever you are, whether at home or an outside location.

The disadvantage is they are not inexpensive – typically $100 to $400. A reputable entertainer can be the party's highlight. Still, if you're on a tight budget, there are better uses for those kinds of funds. One way to save on entertainment is to ask friends and family to help as entertainers. For example, someone you know can paint faces or apply removable tattoos. Or a neighborhood teenager may know how to make some basic balloon animals. Rental costumes of famous characters are available. Remember that using nonprofessional helpers gets more difficult the older the children, and don't expect the neighbor or dad to perform up to the level of an experienced professional.

Consider the ages and attention spans of the guests, in addition to your child's preferences. For example, a clown is usually a good choice for younger children. Still, your child may not like clowns or, for that matter, any performer. Clowns and character actors are usually suitable for ages three to four. Puppet shows, singers, and musicians that can lead the children in songs are also suitable for younger audiences. Magicians and entertainers that rely on interaction and attentiveness are more appropriate for ages five to seven. Face painters are another excellent choice for ages four to eight, especially during arrival activities and free play. (Be sure that face painters use non-toxic, hypoallergenic, FDA-approved, water-soluble face paints, not typical craft paints like acrylics or poster paints. Remember that even the best face paints still may stain clothes, especially red colors, and even with hypoallergenic paints, allergic reactions may still occur.)

Younger children have a balloon choking risk, so balloon artists are recommended for ages five and older. They should be later in the event, as children usually lose focus on the group once given a balloon sword or an animal to focus on instead. Balloon sculptures and outdoor events don't always mix; freshly cut grass is instant doom for a balloon. Ask the balloon artist to make a few extra swords and flowers as "popper replacements" for children to take when their balloon sculpture doesn't survive the party. Keep these extras out of sight until the children leave.

When considering an entertainer, see if it's possible to see their show beforehand. The most important thing is that they work well with children. For example, a good children's magician does not need to make an actual tiger appear. Instead, look for the performer who knows they are using magic as the venue for the children's entertainment. If unsure about an entertainer, ask for references you can call and talk with. It's a red flag if they can't provide any. Often, other parents you trust may recommend reliable performers.

Be sure to reserve a parking space with easy access for the performer so that they may unload any gear quickly. Have the show indoors so it's easier for children to focus without the usual distractions that come from being outside. For the best "stage," most performers require at least a 6x8 foot space up against a wall with good lighting from the front. Backlighting (like from a glass window or door or track lighting behind the performer) will make it difficult for the children to see and ruin any photographs or video you may want. Have an open space for the children to sit on the floor. This way, it's easier for the children to come up as volunteers and be part of the show. Avoid serving food during entertainment as it's a distraction and risks spills and messes.

With any hired entertainment, have one or two adults continually present during the show to supervise and help with any problems. For example, suppose a problem with a child (or even the entertainer) arises. In that case, the extra adult can help, allowing the other children to enjoy the show. A supervisor can usually double as a great photographer.

If your child is shy, introduce them to the entertainer when they arrive. Ask the entertainer if there are any last-minute requirements or changes. Entertainers may allow your child to participate in or be the show's star. Let the entertainer know beforehand if your child is shy and doesn't want to be the show's star. But don't be surprised if the opposite of what your child typically occurs. For example, the shy child may suddenly want to be the show's star, and the outgoing child may shy away.

Most entertainers adhere to the old saying, "The show must go on." But life happens to professionals also, and they may cancel or not show up. Be sure your entire party doesn't revolve around the entertainer. Have a backup plan such as additional games, activities, or videos. Ask the performer if they can send out a confirmation letter or if they require a contract. As with all contracts, read the fine print.

Guest List

Decide on the number of guests before discussing it with your child and do it in accord with your budget. Start with "absolutely invited" guests such as best friends, close family members (especially ones that can be helpers), and any other essential guests that come to mind. A smaller number of guests who are close to your child is preferable to a few dozen acquaintances. Remember that you don't have to invite everyone, such as the class bully or the child with the "always late" parents.

> ### Quick Tips
> - Invite at least one friend your child sees a lot and feels comfortable around.
> - Invite only as many guests as can fit in your space or venue.

If your child is in preschool, you should make the guest list. If they are ages three to four or above, involve them in the guest list. Children ages five to eight will know who they want to invite. Don't completely cater to your child here, maintain veto power and feel free to limit the number of children you invite. The more children the more difficult overall party management will be. A general rule is to invite the "age plus one." For example, a five-year-old's party would have six guests. The main reason for this rule is that the younger the child, the more attention and supervision they will need. Going above this will make it challenging to keep track of each child's needs and be aware of problems such as shy children, picky eaters, conflicts, etc. If your child is used to being with large groups, such as at daycare or preschool, he can handle a few additional guests. Most homes can accommodate eight to fifteen children at a maximum.

Many school districts have policies for party invitations. Ask the school about any rules. Some may allow you to send invitations to school only if the whole class is invited. Remember that inviting the entire class goes against the "age plus one" rule. It's often better to stick to your ideal guest total and invite the guests your child wants.

Organize your guest list and invitations using the Guest List template at the back of this book. If you have names, addresses, and notes you'd like to keep, retain old guest lists for future parties.

Invitations

Invitations can set the tone and introduce the theme of the party. Consider different types of invitations and which one would go best with the party theme. You can also combine types of invitations. For example, sending an e-mail to "save the date" with a paper invitation sent later could work well, and paper is always a nice touch. Some good websites for invitation ideas are Etsy™, Pinterest™ and Vistaprint™. There are also several card-making software and clip art programs available.

Some websites send invitations by e-mail, but gathering all the parents' e-mail addresses may be challenging. Direct e-mails are useful for contacting unfamiliar parents. Avoid social media invitations as most parents won't take them seriously and many things can go awry here. Resources for getting parent contact information include other parents, social media, PTA or your school's directory.

Mail invitations two to three weeks before, allowing you enough time to collect RSVPs and make your final preparations. If the party is during a busy activity season, consider sending them earlier with an additional reminder.

Most parents should know that when the invitation lists their child's name only, that siblings are not invited. But sometimes this message isn't clear, and some families assume that bringing younger and older siblings is okay, and it usually works out alright. If you have limited space and resources, consider putting "siblings not invited" on the invitation. Keep in mind too many unexpected guests can be a problem if you don't have plenty of space. And problems can arise if there is too much of an age gap between a guest's siblings and the rest. For example, significantly younger guests may get in the way and require attention, and older guests may dominate any activities. If you can't accommodate extra siblings, politely mention this when you send the invitation or accept the RSVP. Use your best judgment and be ready to turn people away with a smile if needed. If accommodating extra children, have a few extra favor bags on hand.

Along the same lines, neighbors, acquaintances, and distant family members may assume they can just show up. RSVP time is when you should confirm if the parents are staying or dropping off. If needed, draw firm social boundaries with problematic ex-spouses and significant others. The party atmosphere can quickly deteriorate if there are too many people at the home or venue or if there is a problematic guest adult.

An invitation should provide the following:

- Occasion (Fifth Birthday)
- The party host (your child's first and last name to avoid confusion... "Which Joseph?")
- Day of the party
- Date of the party
- Start time and End time (pickup time). Specify if the start and end times are considered sharp; otherwise, some parents may assume it's flexible when it's not.
- Party location and address (with a map or described landmarks if needed)
- RSVP deadline
- Your cell phone number and e-mail address
- Rain plan (if outdoors)
- Include any requests or special details like "bring a swimsuit," "lunch provided," etc.

Unless you want to spend a small fortune on postage, stick to mailing standard card-style invitations or utilize e-mail invitations. If hand-delivering the invitations, have a little fun with them – be creative and do things like tying the invitation to a rubber ducky for a Pool or Beach Party or attaching a message in a bottle or a plastic eye patch to the invitation for a Pirate Party. If making invitations and your child is over five, try to involve them in the process.

Some other ideas for creative homemade invitations include:

- Purchase white pencil boxes or school boxes and paint or stencil graphics on the sides. Place the party info inside, along with a favor.
- From a coloring book or clip art, find and make a copy of a large number, character, animal, or item that fits with the party's theme. Enlarge it and write in all the party information. Photocopy it and send it in colored envelopes.
- Make reprints of a photo of your child and glue it to the invitation. Write "Look who's turning 2!" and write the party specifics on the other side.

As you'll need accurate attendance numbers, avoid the phrase "Regrets only" on the invitation. Request RSVPs by phone or e-mail one to two weeks before the party and follow up on any unanswered RSVPs. You should have a final headcount for both children and adults a week prior to the date. Don't be upset if someone RSVPs "no" or has a last-minute cancellation. Be courteous – life happens to all of us.

Phone calls between parents can accomplish a few things at once, and sometimes things are best done through direct conversation. Some parents may ask for gift ideas, so have a few ideas ready and avoid duplicates. (Avoid gift registries as they come off as pretentious for children.) Depending on circumstances, you may want a "no gifts please" party, but it's not advisable as many parents feel uncomfortable not bringing anything. Phone calls give you a chance to answer parents' questions like whether the invitee's little brother or sister can come along. This is an excellent opportunity for parents to let you know of any potential restrictions like food allergies, dietary restrictions, face paint sensitivities, or latex allergies (balloons). Some children with dietary restrictions may want to bring their own snacks, and parents of children with allergies may want to be present with an Epi-pen™. Be sure to get the guests' parents' cell phone numbers if an issue arises during the party or for any last-minute changes.

Lastly, creating the invitations can also be a learning experience for your child. It's a chance to teach them about creating results and party etiquette by not talking or bragging about the party at school or around people (adults or children) who are not invited.

Party Supplies

While the party atmosphere is everything, the details and number of decorations are less important for younger children. So, a little fun and creativity combined with children's imaginations goes a long way. And you don't have to spend a fortune.

> **Quick Tips**
> - When ordering supplies online, allow enough time for delivery and the possibility of lost packages.
> - If needed, borrow things like foldable tables, extra chairs, and ice chests from family and friends.

One of the easiest ways to decorate is to buy a complete and themed partyware set, which usually has matching tablecloths, plates, cups, and napkins. You can purchase fun partyware like plastic champagne glasses, colored paper plates, or fun-shaped straws. Everything doesn't need to match or coordinate – you can mix and match supplies. Cheaper green paper plates and more expensive dinosaur movie-printed cups make a nice set. Fun-shaped ice cube trays are a nice touch. (Avoid sharp objects like knives, toothpicks, and paper drink umbrellas.) Don't overdo the theme because you, your child, and your guests will get "over-themed." For example, a Teddy Bear party with Teddy decorations, games, favors, and cake served on Teddy plates is a whole bunch of Teddy.

Even if you have a great party store nearby, check out other sources like dollar stores, trick shops, discount grocery stores, and online party stores. Not only will you find a good selection of supplies, but also many ideas for themes. You may often find what you need, and the prices may be less than at a party store.

Some online companies are efficient and ship the next day, while others may take weeks. Keep an eye on shipping charges and keep an eye on where the items are shipping from. A shipping charge may be reasonable if ordering all the party supplies from one website. On the other hand, if you're ordering a $3 package of small paper plates, you may pay more for shipping than for the item itself. If you are making items or decorations, order them ahead of time.

Another idea is to use some things you use for other occasions. If you have a quality banner that says, "Happy Birthday," you can use it year after year but hang it in a different area each year. If you have leftover supplies from the previous year, make life easier and use them in the following years. For example, use leftover green streamers from a dinosaur party the next year as seaweed for an under-the-sea party. Consider donating still-packaged supplies to women's shelters, homeless shelters, Goodwill, or the Salvation Army – it may make a difference to a family.

Decorations

Decorations are another place where you shouldn't stress or overdo it. Themed paper goods and party supplies may be most of what you'll need. Take some time to look around your home and see what hits you creatively. Think to yourself, "What can I do with this" for ideas that fit easily with your theme. Making decorations can be fun, but sometimes it's much easier and usually less expensive to buy certain things for a party instead of making them. Better yet, make some things that lend themselves to fun projects with the birthday child beforehand, and buy others that would be necessary, central to the theme, or challenging to make in time for the party. Consider having a place for photos, maybe near the entrance or the main area of the party.

> **Quick Tips**
> - Go for simple decorating ideas that make an impact.
> - Personalization makes an impression.
> - Bigger isn't always better – people remember the fun.

Traditional centerpieces are optional for kids' parties. Instead, arrange the partyware and cake as the focal point on the table, especially if you are short on table space. On the other hand, sometimes a centerpiece lends itself to a theme, such as flowers or plants for a jungle party or a cowboy hat for a wild west party. Use a few helium-filled balloons, a single giant balloon, or a canopy of streamers over the table to create height. Create a decorative table by using a few differently colored, semi-translucent plastic tablecloths arranged at angles to each other.

One nice touch is to have a banner. You can buy inexpensive banners or go online and create more expensive ones customized with names and photos. After you've cleaned up after the party, you can keep the banner up for a few days as a reminder of the special event. Another option is to create a piece of memorabilia by getting a banner that guests and families can add best wishes to and sign – this works especially nicely for first birthdays.

Streamers are good, inexpensive, and adaptable decorations. If both ends are attached to something, twisting them as you go always looks better, but hanging them flat takes less time. You can use a few or many of them with different effects. Hanging a few in a cluster or over a doorway can add variety and make the decorated area look more significant and complete. Using a lot of them, such as hanging them from the lighting fixture (avoiding hot bulbs) and attaching them to the corners of the ceiling or attaching them from the ceiling to the corners of the table in a canopy fashion, can make a huge impact, but this will take more time and may require help. One alternative is to buy pre-made mylar or paper streamer curtains. A streamer curtain over a doorway helps create an entrance or boundary to a party area.

If opting for confetti, use oversized paper confetti. You may be able to find confetti in shapes that fit with the theme. Scattering a bit on the tables will dress things up but avoid having it on the table with the food. Avoid plastic, rigid, or smaller confetti. Always avoid glitter.

Balloons instantly create a festive atmosphere and are the definitive party decoration. There are the standard 11-inch latex balloons, larger 17-inch latex balloons, mylar balloons (the foil-looking ones), and helium-filled or not. Helium-filled balloons are available in party stores, grocery stores, and florists. However, helium has become a bit scarcer and pricier in recent years. Use a combination of regular and helium-filled balloons, each for different things, for the best effect. More formal, larger events lend themselves to big balloon arches, but these are usually just too much for children's parties.

Helium-filled latex balloons float for about a day or two, so pick them up early on party day. When ordering helium-filled balloons, try to call ahead, verify stock, and order the balloons in advance. There is a product called Hi-Float™, which is a liquid substance put into latex balloons to increase float time. It usually costs an additional fee per balloon, but they'll float for two to three days. Helium-filled mylar balloons will float for days or even weeks. You can rent or buy helium tanks and fill the balloons yourself. Still, it depends on your time, and they are typically of lower quality than store-bought balloons.

Be careful when transporting helium-filled balloons. If ordering a lot of balloons, weigh them down in the back seat to not block your rear view. Make more than one trip to the store or borrow someone's van or SUV if needed.

There are different things you can do with helium-filled balloons. Letting some balloons float up to the ceiling with differing lengths of long ribbons is a nice effect, especially for the corners of a room. Create bunches like a bouquet using an odd number of balloons at different heights. Placing these strategically on tables, corners of rooms, and keeping the balloons in the party area will help define "party boundaries" for the children. Party stores carry pre-made balloon weights or use food cans wrapped in colored paper, plastic, or foil. Creative items or favors used as balloon weights make great giveaways.

Regular, non-helium balloons are great as balloon bunches or bouquets where height isn't needed. Tie an odd number of regular balloons with different standard or curling ribbon lengths. Hang them on the backs of chairs, over a doorway, or from ceiling fixtures so long as they are not near ceiling fans or lighting.

There are a few cautions that come with balloons. Even though it may seem harmless and funny, don't inhale helium. Be mindful of the environment, and don't release helium balloons into the atmosphere – attach a weight to them so they don't float away. Uninflated or broken balloon pieces create a choking hazard for small children. Immediately discard any deflated balloons or balloon pieces. Latex allergies are becoming more common. If guests have latex allergies, play it safe and go with a few mylar balloons and streamers.

Birthday Child Siblings

The goal here is to keep the siblings' relationship harmonious, especially those close in age. Remember that just because it's one child's birthday doesn't mean that siblings won't want attention or at least acknowledgment.

In general, birthday siblings fall into one of three groups. Some want to be involved in the party as helpers, some want to be just another guest, and others may wish to have little or no part in it. You'll have to judge where your other children are here. If they want to help, they can help with greeting guests, help with refreshments, help with activities or games, and pass out favor bags at the end. Sometimes if you assign one thing to them, they'll gladly take it on as "their thing."

Some children may not be interested in the party and want to play with their friends instead but may wish to experience the excitement at home altogether. One way to achieve a happy medium here is to invite one of their best friends and have a separate play area if their interest drifts away from the party.

When there is a lot of sibling rivalry, remind your children often that while a birthday focuses on a specific individual, it's also everyone else's chance to celebrate the birthday child's presence in everyone else's lives – to say thank you to them. And remind them that when their birthday comes, it will be time for their celebration. To provide the sibling with some acknowledgment, give them a small "un-birthday" gift. Also, give them (and their friend if invited) a goody bag early in the day to help defuse things. For "no win" situations, consider sending them to a friend's house to play.

Some people pay teenagers to help, which may work with the proper teenager, but it's often not a good idea. Often, they are too shy or self-conscious, easily distracted, or just uninterested. Sometimes it's best to let them do their own thing.

Kids with Special Needs

Things can go awry with children with physical, cognitive, emotional, or social limitations. Some guests may have invisible disabilities that other children may not be aware of. Some important things to help differently abled children during playtime are supervision, effective communication, and safety first.

An adult, trusted caregiver, or parent should always supervise a child with special needs. Use visual messages such as post notes with phrases such as "Don't Touch!" or "Off Limits!" on any other potential source of injury, such as stoves, kitchen drawers, etc. Set playtime rules in clear, simple language and gently repeat them if necessary. Designate the party area from the rest of the home with streamer curtains or signs. Avoid noisy environments that can disturb some special needs children and make communicating difficult.

Age-By-Age

The First Birthday party is really a celebration of the anniversary of your becoming a parent. Realistically, a one-year-old will have no idea of what's going on. Many families skip the traditional birthday party here altogether and make this an adult event. If inviting couples with other one or two-year-olds, keep the party under an hour to accommodate nap times. Have a completely baby-proofed room with extra supplies for the infants. Simple activities are fine here, such as blowing bubbles or singing songs. As "First Birthday" is the theme, don't bother purchasing a ton of themed partyware. Avoid latex balloons, as popped balloons are a choking hazard.

Be prepared for a full range of emotions and an occasional meltdown with two-year-olds. One way to avoid conflict is to put away toys before a crowd of children arrives. Most two-year-olds do parallel play and like to work with their hands. Choose clay, water, or coloring activities, and be prepared for them to make a mess. Keep the gift opening for the family after the party, as most young guests will want to take toys home. Avoid latex balloons, as popped balloons are a choking hazard. Keep the party to about 60 to 90 minutes.

Around age three, children start to understand what parties are about. They have some experience in groups from preschool, daycare, etc. While they may like playing with other children for short periods, most have yet to get the hang of cooperating with others, which varies from child to child. Some may be shyer than others, so don't expect too much from the kids. Three-year-olds often like imitation games like Simon Says and singing and circle activities. Keep the gift opening for the family after the party, as most threes will want to take the toys home. Avoid latex balloons, as popped balloons are a choking hazard. Keep the party to about 90 minutes.

Age four is when imagination, energy, and a short attention span kick in. Keep things moving with physical activities and short games. They've discovered more laughter at this age and often go for silly songs.

Five-year-olds' imaginations have kicked in, and they enjoy make-believe games. They have developed fine motor skills and understand right and left, so they do well with crafts and games like Hokey Pokey. Some children may still have trouble taking turns at this age, so be prepared with activities involving the entire group simultaneously. Keep the party to about two hours.

Children age six to eight have formed friendships, which may be important for them. Also, they have specific ideas about what they want for their party. Ages six and up can do well with parties at locations outside of the home. They have a sense of fairness, understand rules for organized games, and often go for games with mysteries, clues, puzzles, etc.

Safety First

Stock band-aids, ice packs, and tissue, and have a standard household First Aid kit. Child-proof the party area: cover electrical outlets, tape down electrical wires, and lock or disconnect electronics like electronics and stereos you won't be using. Protect or remove sharp objects and expensive breakables. Tie back draperies and secure tempting exercise equipment. For children under 3, enclose the party area with gates, leave space for running, preferably near the free play area, and cordon off entrances to swimming pools.

> **Quick Tip**
> If you expect the unexpected, it can't sneak up and surprise you.

Lock up or separate any pets from the children. While pets may be part of your family, they should be locked or secured in another room before and during the party to avoid problems and distractions. Some children are allergic to animals; others may fear even the most gentle or small animals. Others may not know it's not okay to pull on an animal's tail or pet an animal too aggressively. Some pets may be afraid of strangers who have entered the home, whether they are small children, strange adults, or costumed entertainers. Locking up pets is a must when an entertainer brings animals as part of the show.

Immediately throw away any broken or deflated balloons or stick with Mylar balloons. Avoid latex balloons if there is concern about latex allergies. Be sure foods do not present a choking or allergy hazard. If doing crafts, be careful of small items that could be choking hazards for smaller children. Any wood pieces should be smooth to prevent splinters or cuts. Be sure that an adult supervises craft time.

Have more adult supervision than you may need, especially if at a location. Extra adults can help with an upset child so the rest of the party can continue. If holding the party at a public pool, ensure the presence of a certified lifeguard and enough adults to supervise every child. See if there are any restrictions on pool toys and flotation devices. If outdoors, remember to bring sunscreen and insect repellant and have a backup plan in case of bad weather. Letting the children go outside or run around makes it difficult for them to calm down when it's time. Be vigilant during outdoor games so things don't degenerate into free-form tackles. A little refereeing can make all the difference.

The Party Schedule

There are a few reasons to have a party schedule, even if it's simple. It provides a structure to the event, allows you to organize, and gives a sense of security and direction. Some types of parties need very little scheduling, such as going to a sporting event. If an event is at a location such as a kid-themed restaurant, schedules are still helpful, even if they are simple as start, cake, and end times. Write the activities in the day's plan and your contingency activities on a 3"x5" card or list them in your phone. Keep the card in your pocket – it will help you not to forget anything.

The typical party will last from one to two hours, depending on the age of the children. Some people prefer shorter parties of around an hour to make things easier for the parents and reduce the chance that children may get fussy. Still, two hours is the preferred and standard birthday party time.

Time may pass quickly, and keeping the children interested is essential. Change activities about every 20 minutes and change the pace of the activities. To keep things lively, schedule short breaks. Be prepared to eliminate a break if things are going well or create a short break when needed. Change the schedule around if you must. For example, move a quiet activity around in the program as a peaceful break if required. If you are running behind, make up time when serving refreshments, when cutting the cake, by cutting gift opening short by saving presents from family for later, or, if needed, by eliminating gift opening altogether.

Some people avoid unplanned time at the party for fear that the children will get unruly. But 15-20 minutes of arrival time activities at the beginning and the end of the party works well to transition the children into and out of the party. Don't be surprised if this is when they interact with each other the most. Have a craft/activity table as a safety net for when the kids need a little downtime.

Children can gobble up food in minutes, so only plan a little time for refreshments. If hiring live entertainment, provide refreshments for the children before or after the show. If the children eat or drink during the show, their enthusiasm, the show, and your carpet may suffer! Typically, after the entertainment, have the birthday child sit at the head of the table. At the same time, everyone sings a round of "Happy Birthday," the birthday child makes a wish, and blows out the candles.

Here is a typical two-hour party schedule:

- 15-20 minutes - greet arrivals, arrival activities, free play area
- 30-45 minutes - organized games or entertainment
- 15-20 minutes - refreshments
- 20-30 minutes - additional organized activities or present opening
- 15-20 minutes - free play, revisit arrival activities

Don't stress if the schedule is not going as planned – it won't. An activity expected to take 10 minutes might take 30. Be prepared for an activity to fall flat after only five minutes. Have a few contingency games and activities if one isn't working right. Avoid letting it get to the point where kids become frustrated or upset.

Just Before the Party

The day before, call and confirm your extra help for the party, both hired and volunteer. Take care of last-minute details and errands so you don't have to leave the house on party day. Along the same lines, don't leave anything to cook or prepare on the day of the party.

When your child is asleep the night before, decorate their bedroom with streamers, etc. (but no balloons or other risky items here). What a great way to wake up!

Be ready early. Putting away toys not intended for use during the party helps keep the children from getting distracted. Lock up or separate any pets from guest areas. Hang a cluster of balloons on the mailbox or place a party sign in the yard. Set the cake and other partyware out as decorations. Hang a curtain of streamers or place gateways in doorways to rooms off-limits to children. Make a final pass throughout the entire party environment.

Arrival Activities and Free Play

Make guests feel special by greeting them attentively upon arrival and giving them a name badge. It's essential here to "operate the door" (or have someone else do it for you) – to answer the door promptly and provide initial instructions such as writing their name on their favor bag. A delay here can hamper a child's enthusiasm for the party if he's ignored or left standing at the doorway at the outset. Also, this is an opportunity to gently remind parents when the party ends so they know when to pick up their child. It's also a good chance to let kids know your ground rules early on. For example, you might announce, "Just three rules, kids: no jumping on the furniture, take turns, and 'please' and 'thank you.'" This can save you untold trouble later. If you have an uninvited guest that you cannot accommodate and need to turn them away, do it at the time of arrival, do it with a smile, and give them a gentle explanation as to why, such as limited space, etc.

Expect early arrivals about 15 minutes prior to the start time and allow for late arrivals 15 minutes after the start time. Direct children into an arrival activity and free play area as they arrive. Arrival activities can act as icebreakers, so keep them open-ended. A well-planned and set-up arrival activity center and free play area will keep the children busy until everyone arrives, allow shy children to adjust to each other and unfamiliar surroundings, and allow for a transition to group activities.

Quick Tips
- Arrival sets the tone for the party.
- Greet guests with a smile.
- Don't act or appear rushed, even if you are.

Arrival activities allow them time to explore and acclimate to the party location. Use this introduction time to write out the child's name tag and write their name on their Goodie Bag. Arrival activities and free play areas should have simple activities accessible to the children before, throughout, and after the party. They should be able to accommodate individual children or groups of children. If a particular child is shy or doesn't want to participate in a group activity, let him stay doing arrival activities or in the free play area until he is comfortable.

Good activity centers include puzzle books, dot-to-dot, mazes, picture drawing, face painting, making and decorating name tags or party hats, and inexpensive games such as a foam dart board, bean bag toss, or a ring toss. You can set up other simple games using supplies you may already have or can borrow. Arts & crafts should be easy for the children to do. Avoid crafts that require messy glue. Use washable paints and markers to avoid staining skin or clothes. Beads and cord crafts, modeling clay, painting with water books, handprints in clay, and pipe cleaner projects are popular crafts with which most children are familiar. These can also serve as party favors the children can take home. Cover a table with a large piece of white paper like a tablecloth, tape it down at the corners/edges, and let the children color right on it. Many websites have printable crafts such as paper airplanes, origami, etc.

Consider having a free play area set up near the arrival activities area. Some children like individual play so much that getting them into group activities or games may be difficult. Some parents have some of their child's toys available for free play. If opting for this, do not use any of your child's favorite toys. Choose ones appropriate for free play, like toy cars, stacking toys, dolls, or party favors that introduce the party's theme. Be sure to get your child's okay on any toys used in free play.

Sometimes a popular but short video playing near the arrival activity area is a good idea. Play one you own, can stream, or even borrow from the local library. Be sure, though, to start the video so that it ends fifteen minutes or so before the next activity. That way, it comes to a natural conclusion and allows you to move on to the next activity quickly. Avoid video games here and throughout the rest of the party. It's difficult to distract children from video games in favor of other activities. Consider putting the entire video console and video games out of sight for the whole party. Have more than one or two activities ready in case one goes quickly or if there are a few latecomers.

Be sure your arrival activities and free play areas are within your view, or have an extra adult supervise. Try not to have it too far away from the other activities so that if a shy child spends time at the activity center, they are still part of the party.

Games and Group Activities

Unlike arrival activities, group activities provide a chance for children to interact. They can be one of the best parts of a party and will allow kids to let off steam and burn up energy.

Start with a game that allows the children to interact with each other, gets the kids active, and ties into the party's theme. Move on to more organized and dynamic games in a commonsense order. For example, if a game requires kids to take turns, follow it with some physical challenge or activity that all of them can do simultaneously. End with a quieter game to help them wind down just before refreshments.

Remember your audience. You will only have children's attention briefly, so keep game instructions short and sweet. Along the same lines, don't make games up. Instead, use familiar games and adapt them to the party's theme. Older, simpler, and classic games work best for younger children. Some of these games may be new for younger audiences. For example, make a variation of Pin the Tail on the Donkey by creating a game from poster board and construction paper that ties in with your party theme, such as "Stick the tail on the Dinosaur." Other activities  include breaking a piñata, charades, Button, button, who's got the button?, duck-duck-goose, freeze dance, hot potato, keep up the balloon, musical chairs, red rover, relay races, scavenger hunts, Simon Says, and three-legged race.

Remember that children will have varying skill levels in different areas, and some may have disabilities. Be on hand to help kids have success at a given activity. Because a children's party is just that, it should not be considered a sports contest. While it's okay to have winners and losers in games, it's not okay to have the activity be too competitive and make them feel bad. If an activity requires teams, count off 1, 2, 1, 2 to determine teams. Only use blindfolds with older children.

Be flexible. Have some contingency games ready if needed. If a parent brings a guest's siblings, have a few games in reserve for children a bit younger and a bit older than the birthday child and most guests. Don't expect all the children to participate in an activity. Be ready to let an activity go longer if it's going well. If a game is too challenging, not challenging enough, or not keeping the children's attention, cut it short and move on. The schedule is only a guideline. The critical point is for them to have a good time, not necessarily sticking to the schedule.

Keep safety in mind and use double-sided tape instead of pins. Have extra prizes for needs such as surprise guests and tiebreakers. Fill a box or basket with everything you'll need for each game or activity and put it right where the action will occur.

Refreshments

You will often have three groups of guests – babies, children, and adults. Rather than create extensive menus for everyone, rely on standard, age-appropriate snacks for the youngest children and familiar favorites for the guest children and adults. Some food is always a necessity, but it's lower on the list of priorities for kids than games, opening presents, and singing "Happy Birthday." Also, don't worry about nutrition – it is a party.

> ### Quick Tips
> - If short on time, order groceries online.
> - Allow time for a last-minute run to the grocery store if something doesn't get delivered.

Party food can range from just cake and ice cream for children to full meals for children and adults. Whether to serve a full meal depends on the time of day, the type of party and its expectations, and the number of guests.

Tradition dictates that cake and ice cream are essential, but serving only cake and ice cream can result in too much sugar and insufficient food. Plan to have some kid-friendly snacks – they are easy, less expensive, and popular with kids. Go with individually packaged items like string cheese, granola bars, cheese and crackers, and fruit snacks. What doesn't get used at the party can be used for future snacks and lunches.

If serving a full meal, don't overextend. To optimize time and save money, strike a balance between prepared, delivered, and homemade foods. Make the foods you enjoy making and buy prepared foods that are difficult to make and store. For example, make your family recipe for potato salad the day before, and buy the macaroni and cheese. If cooking at home, opt for foods someone can make a day or two ahead. If you don't like to cook or are short of time, rely more heavily on prepared or catered food.

Making food at home usually costs less than buying prepared foods, but not always. When looking at prepared or catered foods, consider the quality for the price paid. Catering a tray of Italian beef or fried chicken for a large group of adults may be worth the time saved. Use caterers you are familiar with and trust.

If your budget allows, another option is taking the guests out to eat, especially if the party is at a location. There are kid-themed and kid-friendly restaurants. These include pizzerias and ice cream parlors, and this is whether the main party activities are taking place at home or at a restaurant. Pizza restaurants sometimes have expanded menus and can deliver almost anywhere, including parks, schools, etc. Even if eating out, have a few individually packaged snacks for fussy eaters.

Some party themes cry out for certain foods. While you can serve obvious foods for a party with a Cinco de Mayo theme, be creative and give classic favorites a personal twist for others. Make party-themed sandwiches and cut them with cookie cutters shaped like characters or objects. When serving pasta, use fun shapes like animal shapes. If ordering pizza, ask the pizzeria to make it into a heart or other shape, and ask them to cut it into small squares (party style).

Child-safe foods are usually soft, bite-sized, and suitable for small hands. Good choices include animal crackers or other small cookies, applesauce, small pieces of banana, black olives, carrots with ranch dressing, cheese cubes or string cheese, cheese spreads, chicken nuggets, chips, cinnamon buns, cookies, crackers, crescent rolls, dry cereal like Cheerios™, finger sandwiches, fruit roll-ups, Goldfish™ crackers, graham crackers, green beans, Jell-O Jigglers™, macaroni & cheese, pasta, cheese pizza,  Popsicles™, French fries, Tater Tots™, nachos, pancakes, pasta, pretzels, pudding, Rice Krispie Treats™, miniature waffles, and yogurt.

Make drinks exciting. Mix milk with chocolate or strawberry flavors. Add a few drops of food coloring to juices or seltzer. But be mindful of drinks that may stain. Clear sodas and juices like apple juice, lemonade, lemon-lime soda, and water are better choices than drinks with red dyes. Plan on at least one to two drinks per guest. Juice boxes are always easier to manage than cups. Write names on the cups or juice boxes to avoid mixed-up drinks. Serve beverages without caffeine as it can make children excitable. Be sure to have a few milk alternatives available for any lactose-intolerant guests.

While older children will know if they are allergic to certain foods, younger ones may not. Ask parents about any food allergies, dietary restrictions, or requests at the time of the RSVP. Allergies to egg, milk, soy, wheat, peanuts, and tree nuts represent 90% of food allergies in children. Strawberries are also a common allergen. Fish and shellfish are other common food allergies, although usually more common in adults. Allergic reactions to food range from mild to life-threatening, and include sneezing, stomach cramps, rash, hives, swelling, vomiting, difficulty breathing and anaphylaxis. Be aware that some allergenic foods hide in other prepared foods, such as peanuts in hard-shell candies and trail mix – just avoid anything with peanuts.

Avoid very hot or spicy foods like fireball candies, jalapeño peppers, etc., even with foods served to adults to prevent children from getting into them. Avoid foods that may be choking hazards with smaller children. Don't serve fruits or raw vegetables cut into coin shapes, grapes, cherries, apples (unless sliced), nuts, hot dog pieces, popcorn, hard candies, or raisins to children under five.

Have food on hand for fussy eaters. Some children may not like tomato sauce, so have some classic macaroni and cheese on hand. Try to provide some alternatives – for instance, non-dairy ice cream for lactose-intolerant kids, a gluten-free item, and vegetarian and sugar-free options. You may not need these options, but not having one or two on hand can create a crying child.

If many adults or parents are attending, you'll need extra food. You'll want to avoid making too many kinds of foods. Choose foods that are both kid and grown-up friendly, as some can be upgraded or expanded for adults. Cater a tray of mostaccioli that both kids and adults can have. If ordering cheese pizza for the children, order a small pizza with all the fixings for the adults. Add fancier cheeses, crackers, and a wider selection of fresh fruit, vegetables, dips, and crackers to your party trays. Make it easy on yourself with easy-to-make or cater food, sticking to standard fare such as BBQ sandwiches, bratwurst, chips & guacamole/salsa, deviled eggs, fried chicken, hamburgers, humus & pita, Italian beef, loaded nachos, meat & cheese trays, mostaccioli, pizza, potato salad, raw fruit/veggie trays with dip, submarine sandwich trays, and chicken wings. Have a separate area for adult foods children may not be interested in.

Lastly, you won't have time to cook during the party, so everything should be ready to serve before – you want to be with the kids rather than in the kitchen. Keep refreshments in or near the kitchen to aid in cleanup. Have some paper towels or wipes ready to clean up after activities and before and after refreshments. If you've followed the advice in this guide and started to hear a few whines from the guests, you'll know it's time for food!

Cake and Ice Cream

The birthday cake is often the center of the birthday ceremony. This is a good opportunity to involve the birthday child, asking them to help make, pick out, or describe what kind of cake they would like. It's up to you and your child to make or buy a cake.

If making a cake, look online, in the bakery aisle of the grocery store, and at craft or hobby stores for things you can add to dress up a cake following the party's theme. Only use decorations designed for cakes or child-safe toys as cake decorations. You can tint the batter and icing if desired. If tinting icing, use lighter or pastel shades, as deep colors like red can stain little faces, tongues, clothes, and furniture. If making a cake, you can make it days ahead and freeze it.

Bakery departments in large grocery stores often have a good selection of decorated and customizable cakes on short notice. Cakes from bakeries are usually of higher quality but may cost more. Sometimes, you can leave a party favor or napkin with the baker so they can closely match the cake colors to the party's theme and decoration colors.

Many parents use cupcakes instead of traditional cakes. There are many upsides to using cupcakes. They are ideal for smaller children and allow you to save a larger cake for a family party later. They are easier to make and decorate than standard cakes. Portions are predetermined. You won't have to provide plates and forks, and you can avoid messy cake cutting (but let the birthday child pick the first cupcake instead of making the first cut). You can have more than one cupcake flavor for fussy eaters. They can be decorated as individual mini birthday cakes or set together and frosted as one larger pull-apart birthday cake with a shape matching the theme. They can also be displayed on a cupcake tower stand.

Another idea is to use cupcake cones. Make a boxed cake batter as directed. Fill flat-bottomed ice cream cones (plain or colored) 3/4 full of cake batter and bake them standing up on a cookie sheet or in a cupcake pan (cone and all) according to the directions for cupcakes. The batter will rise to fill the cone. Cool completely. Frost and decorate as desired.

The cake is usually the centerpiece of the refreshment table, but feel free to display the cake on a serving platter, possibly on a separate table, surrounded by partyware in a display. Have the candles, matches, knife, and plastic utensils ready but out of the children's reach. Put the candles on the cake just before lighting them and singing. As lighted candles can be dangerous, always be in control and remove them before serving. Have a cup of water to douse them as each is removed from the cake; otherwise, ribbons, decorations, and ponytails can ignite. Avoid sparklers which are much more dangerous than most people think. The birthday child will usually want the first piece.

Have a few flavors of ice cream available as some young children prefer ice cream over cake. Buy ice cream cups, bars, or sandwiches to avoid the work and mess of scooping out ice cream by hand. Ice cream cakes are another excellent option because they almost always signify a special occasion and take care of the cake and the ice cream at the same time.

Gift Opening

Parents have differing opinions about opening presents during a birthday party. Some feel that it is too materialistic, or that a guest's or even the birthday child's feelings might be hurt if the present is a duplicate or doesn't create a favorable response. Others feel this is the party's highlight and is a logical closing activity. When deciding whether to open gifts during or after the party, consider your child's personality, the number of guests, the age, party time management, and the present level of chaos. For example, if your child is overly focused on gifts, it may be better to get it over with and have him open them as each guest arrives, although this goes against the recommended norm. Advantages of opening gifts near the end of a party include having it be the party's highlight (next to blowing out the candles), and each gift giver gets acknowledged.

Younger children may have desires for the toys themselves, be jealous, or even be embarrassed if the gift is a duplicate or unwanted, or if they forgot to bring a gift. It's difficult for very young children to share new toys, and it's hard for other younger children who are not getting toys to sit and watch. Opening presents is usually best left out of a party for children under five years of age. But if opening gifts for young children, two things that can help here are keeping things moving and giving each child a favor as something to focus on and feel as if they have gotten something also.

Around age five or six, the other children have grown a bit and like to see their gifts opened in addition to wanting to check out the other presents. If you want to open gifts during the party, do it in an orderly, controlled fashion. Have the children sit on the floor, in a circle or a group, and open the presents one by one.

Advantages of opening gifts afterward include extending the party for the birthday child, creating a family component to the party day, allowing you to track who gave which gift more accurately, and avoiding the problem of lost cards and a frenzy of over-excited kids amidst a sea of torn paper. If you are having the party at a venue, it may be better to utilize the time for venue-focused activities instead of gift opening.

This is a great opportunity to teach your child about thanking others. Rehearse your child on thank you speeches for the gifts before the party. Ask an adult helper to record the gifts on the Guest List to keep track of gifts received, making it easy to mention them in Thank You notes. (Some parents tape the card to the gift to keep track of each giver.) That way, you can focus on praising the gift giver, helping elicit appropriate thanks from your child, and greeting any parents that arrive early for pickup. Discard wrapping paper directly into a handy plastic garbage or recycling bag as you go along. Keep it moving to avoid losing the guests' attention – younger children may be unable to sit through a long gift-opening session.

One of the most important things to remember is that gift opening comes secondary to the children's good time. If they are having a great time during a particular activity and it runs into the time scheduled for gift opening, don't worry. Let them continue to have fun and save the gift opening for after the party.

Farewell Activities

Keep the children entertained as parents arrive. Allow children to revisit the arrival activities or free play area. Play games, color pictures, play a popular but short video, or eat more treats. It's often best to do a quieter indoor rather than a louder outdoor activity so that arriving parents don't enter chaos.

Party Favors

Take-home favors and goodie bags have become an expectation and are a great way to thank your guests for attending. Sometimes, it's possible to have the birthday child hand these out to the guests as they leave to learn that it's not just about receiving but giving also.

Provide colorful paper or cellophane bags and have guests write their names on their bags when they arrive. Create all goodie bags and contents the same to avoid jealousy and disappointments. Guests can put any favors, prizes, and completed art projects in their bags throughout the party. Have a couple of extra bags for unexpected guests and make a favor bag for your child and any siblings. Having the bags near the door will remind the children to take them as they leave, keeping them up on a table to keep children from getting into them beforehand.

Stick to a budget here, as the costs of party favors can add up. A reasonable $5 to $15 per bag should cover one or two higher-cost favors (two to five dollars) and a few low-cost items like bracelets, and temporary tattoos. Include one or two things that fit with the party's theme. Avoid cheap, breakable favors that will soon be discarded, especially as their short-lived use won't contribute to the guest's experience. Have a mix of practical favors and fun favors. Practical favors such as tote bags, baseball caps, glitter pens, pencils and pencil cases are often appreciated by the other parents. Gift cards are an emerging trend. Use small denomination cards ($5) to a favorite ice cream shop, movie theater, or bookstore. Although slightly more expensive, decorated boxes or school/pencil boxes can replace paper goody bags. Items used during arrival activities such as crayons, coloring books and crafts can also serve as take-home favors. A photo cube or refrigerator magnet photo holder to display their children's snapshots is a nice touch.

Remember to include some snacks such as prepackaged cookies, cotton candy cones, bubble gum, or wrapped cake pops in the Goodie Bags. If using helium-filled balloons, have them weighted down with a toy or favor, ready to give out to each guest as they leave.

Around eight to ten years of age, children often outgrow the standard favor bags. At these ages, a single large favor tied to the party theme, like fun books such as Hardy Boys® or Goosebumps® Adventures, works well.

Additional Goodie Bag ideas include:

- Sidewalk Chalk
- Noisemakers
- Inflatable Beach Balls
- Jump Ropes
- 3D Puzzles
- Bubble wands
- Temporary Tattoos
- Silly Putty™
- Small Science Kits
- Magic Tricks
- Sunglasses
- Squishies
- Fidget Spinners
- Lego™ kits
- Superhero Masks
- Joke Books
- Activity or Coloring Books
- Small Flashlights
- Paint Palettes
- Lego™ Kits
- Slime Kits
- Stuffed Animals
- Slap Bracelets
- Play-Doh™
- Pokémon™ Cards
- Silly String™
- Keychains
- Backpack Clip Ons
- Headbands
- Hot Wheels™ Cars

After the Party

This is another time to delegate. Have family and friends already arranged to help move back furniture, pack up reusable supplies, and clean. This is also a good teaching opportunity for the birthday child and siblings to learn about teamwork and the responsibility of cleaning up, even if they only do one or two chores. Consider a cleaning or maid service for that day or the next.

Thank You Notes

These are a must and are a classy touch. Many guests will be upset without a Thank You. In addition, writing notes is a great way to teach your child the "Magic of Thank You." Don't make the mistake of thinking that if you spend a lot of money on the party or gave out expensive favors or goodie bags that you don't need to send Thank You's.

It's best to write and send Thank You notes one to three days after the party. But if sending a week or two later, then it's better to send them later than never. An older child can sign his name and, by age six, should be able to write his note. Don't worry about spelling. E-mail thank you notes are acceptable but written "real" notes are always preferred.

One particularly nice touch is to have the adult working as the photographer get at least one picture of each child during the party. Upload photos that night, if possible, to a password-protected photo website (with the parents' permission). Note it in the Thank You cards so the parents and their children can see all the pics from the party. After the party, print them out and include them with the Thank You note.

If you don't have the mailing address for a guest, feel free to ask the parent. E-mail Thank You's are becoming more common but lack the personal touch of a mailed Thank You. If e-mailing, try to make it personal by including personal anecdotes or pictures of the guest with the birthday child. Telephone Thank You's are acceptable but should be reserved for when you have no address or e-mail, or have a pre-existing, personal relationship with the parent. Text messages should be avoided as they are seen as effortless and dismissive.

Lastly, don't forget to send Thank You notes to all the adult helpers and leave favorable reviews online for vendors and entertainers – it will make their day!

Finally

Keep the big picture in mind. Plan and prepare, but don't worry when things don't go as planned. Don't expect everything to be perfect. It won't be. While the guidelines and schedule are important, sometimes the rules must go out the window. And that's okay, so long as they don't go out all at once. So be ready to shift gears when needed. There will always be something you'd do differently if you had it to do over again. Some games you thought would be a big hit will be too easy, complex, or slow. Some food you thought kids would devour won't be.

The good news is that no matter what, the kids are having fun. Usually, they won't know or even care when something doesn't go as planned. Remember that if you are stressed, the kids will also be – but if you are having fun, the kids will also.

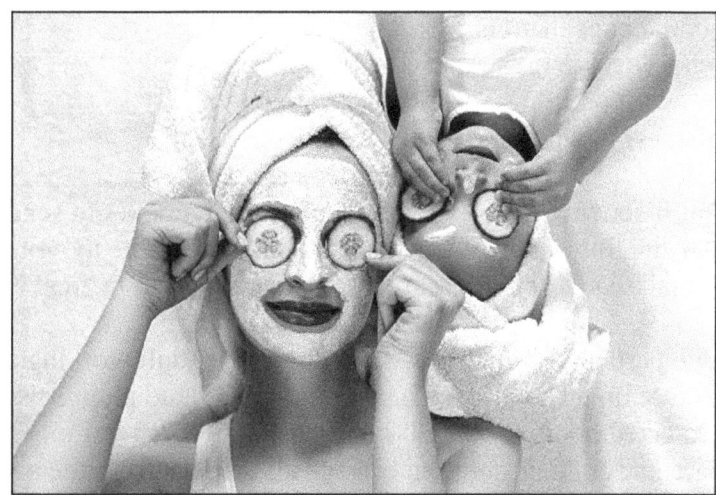

At the end of the day, it's time for *your* treat. Take some time to enjoy a bubble bath, a favorite food, or a cup of herbal tea and congratulate yourself on a job well done!

Kids Party Magic

Planning Guide

Invitation Checklist

- ☐ Occasion: _____

- ☐ Host child's first and last name: _____

- ☐ Day: _____

- ☐ Date: _____

- ☐ Start time: _____

    - ☐ Specify if considered sharp

- ☐ End time (pickup time): _____

    - ☐ Specify if considered sharp

- ☐ Party location/address: _____

    - ☐ Map or described landmarks: _____

    - ☐ Location website: _____

- ☐ RSVP deadline: _____

- ☐ Your cell phone number and e-mail address: _____

- ☐ Rain plan (if outdoors): _____

- ☐ Requests or special details : _____
  _____

www.kidspartymagic.info

Timeline

6-8 Weeks before
- ☐ Pick date & time
- ☐ Choose party theme
- ☐ Set party budget
- ☐ Create guest list
- ☐ Start choosing décor
- ☐ Rent chairs and tables
- ☐ Order invitations
- ☐ Hire entertainment
- ☐ Book Venue

1 Month before
- ☐ Send or email invitations.
- ☐ Order cake
- ☐ Create party schedule
- ☐ Plan games and activities
- ☐ Buy supplies, decorations, & favors
- ☐ Plan menu
- ☐ Create Grocery List
- ☐ Order catering
- ☐ Arrange for extra help on party day
- ☐ _____

1 Week before
- ☐ Order or bake and freeze cake
- ☐ Final headcount to caterer
- ☐ Confirm RSVPs and exact guest count
- ☐ Order helium-filled balloons
- ☐ Finish décor projects, fill loot bags
- ☐ _____

3-4 Days before
- ☐ Make food to be made prior
- ☐ Shop for groceries
- ☐ Music playlist

1-2 Days before
- ☐ Pick up rented items
- ☐ Pick up or finish cake and desserts
- ☐ Defrost cake or frozen foods
- ☐ Refrigerate drinks
- ☐ Clean and child-proof the house
- ☐ Decorate, set up food and gift tables
- ☐ Set out dishes and party supplies
- ☐ Set up arrival activities and games
- ☐ Go to bed early the night before
- ☐ _____

Party day
- ☐ Cook food and prepare refreshments
- ☐ Pick up ordered food
- ☐ Buy ice
- ☐ Pick up helium-filled balloons
- ☐ Last-minute straightening up
- ☐ Balloons on mailbox/party sign on lawn
- ☐ Secure pets
- ☐ _____

Day after party
- ☐ Return borrowed or rented items
- ☐ Clean house
- ☐ Write Thank You notes

www.kidspartymagic.info

Budget

Total Budget Amount: _____

Item	Budget Amount	Actual Cost	Balance	Notes
	Totals			

Shopping List

Deli
- ☐ Cheese tray
- ☐ Deli meat
- ☐ _____

Produce
- ☐ Green beans
- ☐ Carrots
- ☐ _____
- ☐ _____

Fruit
- ☐ Apples
- ☐ Bananas
- ☐ Grapes
- ☐ Watermelon
- ☐ _____
- ☐ _____

Meat & Fish
- ☐ Hot dogs
- ☐ _____

Condiments
- ☐ BBQ Sauce
- ☐ Ketchup
- ☐ Mayonnaise
- ☐ Mustard
- ☐ Salsa
- ☐ _____

Frozen Food
- ☐ Ice cream
- ☐ Ice pops
- ☐ Pizza
- ☐ Chicken nuggets
- ☐ Tater Tots™
- ☐ Ice
- ☐ _____

Canned & Prepared Food
- ☐ Tomato sauce/pasta
- ☐ Macaroni & cheese
- ☐ _____

Beverages
- ☐ Juice boxes
- ☐ Water
- ☐ Soda
- ☐ _____

Snacks
- ☐ Candy
- ☐ Chips
- ☐ Cookies
- ☐ Fruit snacks/chews
- ☐ Goldfish™ crackers
- ☐ Pudding cups
- ☐ Pretzels
- ☐ _____
- ☐ _____

Baking & Spices
- ☐ Cake mix
- ☐ Cake decor
- ☐ Frosting
- ☐ _____

Breads & Cereal
- ☐ Baby cereal
- ☐ Hot dog buns
- ☐ _____

Dairy
- ☐ Milk
- ☐ String Cheese
- ☐ Eggs
- ☐ Yogurt
- ☐ _____

Refrigerated
- ☐ Dip
- ☐ _____

Home
- ☐ Tablecloth
- ☐ Napkins
- ☐ Paper plates and bowls
- ☐ Paper cups
- ☐ Plastic silverware
- ☐ Garbage bags
- ☐ Paper towels
- ☐ Insect repellant
- ☐ First Aid kit
- ☐ Sunscreen
- ☐ Matches or lighter
- ☐ Batteries
- ☐ Wipes
- ☐ Thank You notes
- ☐ Facial tissue
- ☐ Hand soap
- ☐ _____

Decorations
- ☐ Birthday candles
- ☐ Balloons
- ☐ Ribbon
- ☐ Streamers
- ☐ Tape
- ☐ Party hats
- ☐ Piñata & safety bat
- ☐ Party hats
- ☐ Party favors & prizes
- ☐ Activities (puzzles, mazes)
- ☐ Supplies for goodie bags
- ☐ Party sign for lawn/ mailbox
- ☐ _____
- ☐ _____

Gift Wish List

☐ _____

☐ _____

☐ _____

☐ _____

☐ _____

☐ _____

☐ _____

☐ _____

☐ _____

☐ _____

☐ _____

☐ _____

☐ _____

☐ _____

☐ _____

Vendor List

Vendor Name: _____

Product/Services: _____ Quantity: _____

Web Address: _____

Phone: _____ Address: _____

Date Booked: _____ Arrive/Pick up: _____ Return by: _____

Quoted Cost: _____ Deposit Paid: _____ Final Cost: _____

Notes: _____

Vendor Name: _____

Product/Services: _____ Quantity: _____

Web Address: _____

Phone: _____ Address: _____

Date Booked: _____ Arrive/Pick up: _____ Return by: _____

Quoted Cost: _____ Deposit Paid: _____ Final Cost: _____

Notes: _____

Vendor Name: _____

Product/Services: _____ Quantity: _____

Web Address: _____

Phone: _____ Address: _____

Date Booked: _____ Arrive/Pick up: _____ Return by: _____

Quoted Cost: _____ Deposit Paid: _____ Final Cost: _____

Notes: _____

www.kidspartymagic.info

Guest List

Name: _____ Parents: _____

Phone: _____ Email: _____

Address: _____

Requests/Notes: _____

RSVP: ☐ Yes ☐ No ☐ Uncertain   # Guests: _____

Gift: _____   ☐ Thank You Sent

Name: _____ Parents: _____

Phone: _____ Email: _____

Address: _____

Requests/Notes: _____

RSVP: ☐ Yes ☐ No ☐ Uncertain   # Guests: _____

Gift: _____   ☐ Thank You Sent

Name: _____ Parents: _____

Phone: _____ Email: _____

Address: _____

Requests/Notes: _____

RSVP: ☐ Yes ☐ No ☐ Uncertain   # Guests: _____

Gift: _____   ☐ Thank You Sent

Name: _____ Parents: _____

Phone: _____ Email: _____

Address: _____

Requests/Notes: _____

RSVP: ☐ Yes ☐ No ☐ Uncertain   # Guests: _____

Gift: _____   ☐ Thank You Sent

www.kidspartymagic.info

Guest List

Name: _____   Parents: _____

Phone: _____   Email: _____

Address: _____

Requests/Notes: _____

RSVP: ☐ Yes ☐ No ☐ Uncertain   # Guests: _____

Gift: _____   ☐ Thank You Sent

Name: _____   Parents: _____

Phone: _____   Email: _____

Address: _____

Requests/Notes: _____

RSVP: ☐ Yes ☐ No ☐ Uncertain   # Guests: _____

Gift: _____   ☐ Thank You Sent

Name: _____   Parents: _____

Phone: _____   Email: _____

Address: _____

Requests/Notes: _____

RSVP: ☐ Yes ☐ No ☐ Uncertain   # Guests: _____

Gift: _____   ☐ Thank You Sent

Name: _____   Parents: _____

Phone: _____   Email: _____

Address: _____

Requests/Notes: _____

RSVP: ☐ Yes ☐ No ☐ Uncertain   # Guests: _____

Gift: _____   ☐ Thank You Sent

www.kidspartymagic.info

Guest List

Name: _____   Parents: _____

Phone: _____   Email: _____

Address: _____

Requests/Notes: _____

RSVP: ☐ Yes ☐ No ☐ Uncertain   # Guests: _____

Gift: _____   ☐ Thank You Sent

Name: _____   Parents: _____

Phone: _____   Email: _____

Address: _____

Requests/Notes: _____

RSVP: ☐ Yes ☐ No ☐ Uncertain   # Guests: _____

Gift: _____   ☐ Thank You Sent

Name: _____   Parents: _____

Phone: _____   Email: _____

Address: _____

Requests/Notes: _____

RSVP: ☐ Yes ☐ No ☐ Uncertain   # Guests: _____

Gift: _____   ☐ Thank You Sent

Name: _____   Parents: _____

Phone: _____   Email: _____

Address: _____

Requests/Notes: _____

RSVP: ☐ Yes ☐ No ☐ Uncertain   # Guests: _____

Gift: _____   ☐ Thank You Sent

www.kidspartymagic.info

Guest List

Name: _____   Parents: _____

Phone: _____   Email: _____

Address: _____

Requests/Notes: _____

RSVP: ☐ Yes ☐ No ☐ Uncertain   # Guests: _____

Gift: _____   ☐ Thank You Sent

Name: _____   Parents: _____

Phone: _____   Email: _____

Address: _____

Requests/Notes: _____

RSVP: ☐ Yes ☐ No ☐ Uncertain   # Guests: _____

Gift: _____   ☐ Thank You Sent

Name: _____   Parents: _____

Phone: _____   Email: _____

Address: _____

Requests/Notes: _____

RSVP: ☐ Yes ☐ No ☐ Uncertain   # Guests: _____

Gift: _____   ☐ Thank You Sent

Name: _____   Parents: _____

Phone: _____   Email: _____

Address: _____

Requests/Notes: _____

RSVP: ☐ Yes ☐ No ☐ Uncertain   # Guests: _____

Gift: _____   ☐ Thank You Sent

www.kidspartymagic.info

Guest List

Name: _____ Parents: _____

Phone: _____ Email: _____

Address: _____

Requests/Notes: _____

RSVP: ☐ Yes ☐ No ☐ Uncertain   # Guests: _____

Gift: _____   ☐ Thank You Sent

Name: _____ Parents: _____

Phone: _____ Email: _____

Address: _____

Requests/Notes: _____

RSVP: ☐ Yes ☐ No ☐ Uncertain   # Guests: _____

Gift: _____   ☐ Thank You Sent

Name: _____ Parents: _____

Phone: _____ Email: _____

Address: _____

Requests/Notes: _____

RSVP: ☐ Yes ☐ No ☐ Uncertain   # Guests: _____

Gift: _____   ☐ Thank You Sent

Name: _____ Parents: _____

Phone: _____ Email: _____

Address: _____

Requests/Notes: _____

RSVP: ☐ Yes ☐ No ☐ Uncertain   # Guests: _____

Gift: _____   ☐ Thank You Sent

www.kidspartymagic.info

Guest List

Name: _____   Parents: _____

Phone: _____   Email: _____

Address: _____

Requests/Notes: _____

RSVP: ☐ Yes ☐ No ☐ Uncertain   # Guests: _____

Gift: _____   ☐ Thank You Sent

Name: _____   Parents: _____

Phone: _____   Email: _____

Address: _____

Requests/Notes: _____

RSVP: ☐ Yes ☐ No ☐ Uncertain   # Guests: _____

Gift: _____   ☐ Thank You Sent

Name: _____   Parents: _____

Phone: _____   Email: _____

Address: _____

Requests/Notes: _____

RSVP: ☐ Yes ☐ No ☐ Uncertain   # Guests: _____

Gift: _____   ☐ Thank You Sent

Name: _____   Parents: _____

Phone: _____   Email: _____

Address: _____

Requests/Notes: _____

RSVP: ☐ Yes ☐ No ☐ Uncertain   # Guests: _____

Gift: _____   ☐ Thank You Sent

www.kidspartymagic.info

Guest List

Name: _____   Parents: _____

Phone: _____   Email: _____

Address: _____

Requests/Notes: _____

RSVP: ☐ Yes ☐ No ☐ Uncertain   # Guests: _____

Gift: _____   ☐ Thank You Sent

Name: _____   Parents: _____

Phone: _____   Email: _____

Address: _____

Requests/Notes: _____

RSVP: ☐ Yes ☐ No ☐ Uncertain   # Guests: _____

Gift: _____   ☐ Thank You Sent

Name: _____   Parents: _____

Phone: _____   Email: _____

Address: _____

Requests/Notes: _____

RSVP: ☐ Yes ☐ No ☐ Uncertain   # Guests: _____

Gift: _____   ☐ Thank You Sent

Name: _____   Parents: _____

Phone: _____   Email: _____

Address: _____

Requests/Notes: _____

RSVP: ☐ Yes ☐ No ☐ Uncertain   # Guests: _____

Gift: _____   ☐ Thank You Sent

www.kidspartymagic.info

Guest List

Name: _____   Parents: _____

Phone: _____   Email: _____

Address: _____

Requests/Notes: _____

RSVP: ☐ Yes ☐ No ☐ Uncertain   # Guests: _____

Gift: _____   ☐ Thank You Sent

Name: _____   Parents: _____

Phone: _____   Email: _____

Address: _____

Requests/Notes: _____

RSVP: ☐ Yes ☐ No ☐ Uncertain   # Guests: _____

Gift: _____   ☐ Thank You Sent

Name: _____   Parents: _____

Phone: _____   Email: _____

Address: _____

Requests/Notes: _____

RSVP: ☐ Yes ☐ No ☐ Uncertain   # Guests: _____

Gift: _____   ☐ Thank You Sent

Name: _____   Parents: _____

Phone: _____   Email: _____

Address: _____

Requests/Notes: _____

RSVP: ☐ Yes ☐ No ☐ Uncertain   # Guests: _____

Gift: _____   ☐ Thank You Sent

Notes

Acknowledgements

I would like to thank Bob Thomas for bringing me into the world of magic. I am forever indebted to Dr. Lynn Miner for being a life-long mentor and teaching me how magical the art of entertaining children can be. A special thanks goes to Kay Cammon for believing in me as a performer and taking me under her wing. I would like to thank my personal friends Margaret, Ann Marie, Jasmine, and Jennifer for their attention and suggestions to this book. Lastly, I would like to thank all the families and children who I've been fortunate enough to entertain over the years.

About the Author

Dr. Nicholas Rizzo is a longstanding member of the Society of American Magicians and is a life member of the International Brotherhood of Magicians. He has been published in the Linking Ring – the Magazine for the International Brotherhood of Magicians, The Journal of Magic Science, and was featured in Balloon Magic Magazine.

Dr. Rizzo has performed at the Kohler Resort, the Chicago Field Museum, and Six Flags Great America. He has performed for Verizon Wireless, Pfizer, Marriott, ABN Amro, Merck & Co., and others.

This physician knows that in some cultures the phrase "good medicine" means anything that makes you feel better. In other words, medicine alone can't always solve one of our basic needs: to laugh and have fun!

Having performed more than 300 children's shows as a magician, balloon artist, and face painter, he has learned that the little audiences are always the best ones!